Bible Study

7 Sessions for Homegroup
and Personal Use

CW00821712

Isaiah 40-66

Prophet of restoration

John Houghton

CWR

Contents

Introduction

Welcome to the second part of Isaiah's great and glorious prophecy! First of all, a bit of history to set the scene. Isaiah lived as a contemporary of the prophets Hosea and Micah. He prophesied about both immediate and imminent events in Jerusalem from c.740–680BC, during the reigns of the Judaean kings Uzziah, Jotham, Ahaz and Hezekiah. However, this second remarkable phase of his writings addresses a period over 150 years ahead of his time.

Israel, the northern half of the divided kingdom, had long since collapsed to the Assyrians. Soon it would be the southern kingdom's turn, but Judah would not fall to the Assyrian army. In 586BC, within 100 years of Isaiah's death, the Babylonians invaded the south, conquering Jerusalem and destroying the Temple. Mass deportations followed the carnage and it looked like the end of nationhood for God's people. Eking out a sorry existence in the ghettos of Babylon, they were left to reflect on the sins that had brought them to this pitiful state. Their major prophets, Isaiah, Jeremiah and Ezekiel, had spoken the truth. Moses, centuries earlier, had warned them about the consequences of forsaking the living God for the fertility gods of Canaan. Corruption and injustice had become endemic and the prophets were derided and persecuted. It was only a matter of time before they exhausted God's patience, and the punishment, when it came, was just and deserved; God sentenced them to seventy years captivity – a period set to pay off what they owed contractually for all the Sabbaths they had abused and neglected (see 2 Chron. 36:21).

These events must be slotted into the prophetic gap between Isaiah 39 and Isaiah 40. Some have theorised that the change of style and period indicates a different author to Isaiah the son of Amoz and, further, that chapters 55–66 may have been penned by several 'Isaiahs'. However, if we accept that the living God knows the end from the beginning and that Isaiah was inspired by the Holy Spirit, there is no serious reason to doubt the unity of authorship, and this is the position that we shall take in these studies.

God speaks, sometimes centuries in advance, encouraging His people to prepare themselves for the future. Such preparation may be a long-term investment that goes beyond our own lifetimes, but the fruitfulness of the future people of God depends significantly on the faithfulness of the present people of God. Isaiah sees beyond the captivity to a time of remarkable restoration. God's people will return to their homeland; impossible as it might seem, they will rebuild the Temple and re-establish themselves as a nation. They will also rediscover their divine destiny as the Lord's servant; a destiny that will in due course be enshrined in one Man, Jesus of Nazareth, the Messiah and the Saviour of the world.

God is a God of new beginnings, a God of second chances who takes no pleasure in judgment. However, nothing is automatic; deportation may induce remorse and regret but that is insufficient. Profound lessons must be learned if the same errors are to be avoided in the future. Freedom will bring its own challenges; without a change of heart the people could easily fall back into the sins of their ancestors. Isaiah's prophecy provides the counsel and encouragement that they will need when the Lord restores the fortunes of Zion.

God promises restoration even before the judgment has taken place! In wrath, He remembers mercy (see Hab. 3:2). 'Comfort, comfort my people, says your God. Speak tenderly to Jerusalem, and proclaim to her that her hard service has been completed, that her sin has been paid for, that she has received from the Lord's hand double for all her sins' (Isa. 40:1–2). These words introduce us to some of the richest and most profound devotional words ever penned. Their local and contemporary setting reveals truths that are universal and eternal – truths that unfold like the sections of a telescope, enabling us to see far beyond the restoration of God's ancient people. Isaiah predicts the nature and the coming of Christ. He teaches us the principles of spiritual revivals, revealing the pattern of God's dealings in our own lives and churches. He even anticipates the second coming of Jesus and the establishment of a new universe.

The whole of this second part of Isaiah is written in poetic form and hardly surprisingly it has inspired many songs and hymns, not least, Handel's *Messiah*. Indeed, the structure of the prophecy, with its various herald voices, lends itself to operatic drama rather than to a linear logical sequence of ideas. This being so, and to help us with the quantity of material, we shall structure our study around the chief characters, the *dramatis personae*.

We are always somewhere on the roller coaster of life, death and resurrection, whether in our personal lives or in our churches. Whatever our situation, Isaiah has a powerful message for each of us, and never more so if we are praying for and seeking revival. 'Arise, shine, for your light has come, and the glory of the LORD rises upon you' (Isa. 60:1). May you experience the reality of those words as you study Isaiah, the prophet of restoration. With this in mind, we recommend that you read a chapter a day during the course of your studies.

WEEK 1

There is Only One God

Opening Icebreaker

If you had to invent a god, what characteristics would you want him to have, and why? Depending on the size of your group, go round choosing one characteristic each.

Merciful
Forgiving
Steadfast

Bible Readings *Isaiah pg 787*
P831, P832

- Isaiah 40:12–17,21–31
- Isaiah 55:6–13 *P852*
- Isaiah 66:1–2 *P863*

- John 1:1–3,14 *P1253*
- John 4:20–24 *P1258*

Key verse: 'I am the LORD, and there is no other; apart from me there is no God.' Isaiah 45:5

Focus: There is only one Creator and Shepherd, and He is merciful to those who love Him.

Opening Our Eyes

Isaiah contains more direct self-revelation of God than any other book in the Bible, apart from the Gospels. Here God speaks in the first person, telling us that there is no other God but Himself. He is the Origin and the Originator, the first and the last, the eternal and unbounded Creator of all that is and ever will be. Like a builder He calculates and weighs out His materials, but on a monumental scale. The oceans are cupped in the palm of His hand, the skies are but a hand's span, the earth fits into His measuring bucket and He pops the mountains onto His scales. This God orchestrates the unique combination of elements needed to make a planet capable of sustaining the mystery of life. He creates and sustains the galaxies and stars, organising this impossibly vast and complex structure according to His own plans and intents. No one advises Him; no one hinders Him; no word is a lost echo. He speaks and it happens.

There is little point in trying to compare ourselves with Him. Humans, great or small, come and go like summer grass. Our energies wax and wane, but God is for ever, untiring, unchanged by the aeons. The continents, the nations, the islands, are mere dust to the One who sits above the circumference of the earth. As for the world's leaders, well, they are short-lived plants soon to be blown away by the breath of God. Even those raised up by God, the orchestrator of the constellations, are no more than the clay in the potter's hands. They have no more right to express their opinion, let alone argue about their destiny, than does the half-formed pot on the wheel.

So, what of our efforts to localise God and bring to Him our religious offerings? Heaven is His throne, the earth is His footstool. How will you fit Him into a house, even if it be the most grandiose in all the world? The trees and livestock of a whole nation would scarcely make a noticeable offering. How would mere mortals hope to impress the Holy One who inhabits eternity?

These lofty revelations might easily induce despair. Such a God is unknowable; His law is implacable; He has no interest in our puny lives so we must do the best we can without Him. We are impressed, sometimes scared, but not comforted.

However, this is not the whole story. This same almighty God is also the Shepherd of His people. He understands our frailty and treats us as gently as new-born lambs. Our lives may be short, but He promises to carry us from birth to old age. He might inhabit eternity but He also dwells intimately with those who respect His Word with a humble and contrite heart. Rather than standing at a distance in mere admiration, or with false humility turning away muttering that God has no place for us, we are urged to seek God. This is outrageous grace at its best; the One who has no need of us invites us to find Him. If we turn from our evil thoughts and perverse ways, God will freely forgive our wrongdoings. Should we object to this, the Lord reminds us that He doesn't think or act like us. If He says this is how it is then we had better believe it! Joy and peace replace fear and suspicion, and nature itself joins in the applause!

Discussion Starters

1. Part of the spiritual despair in the British psyche is based upon the belief that a personal knowledge of God is impossible to achieve. How would you address this?

2. Politically correct modern-day Pharisees object to Christians' exclusive claims about God or salvation. In what ways do Isaiah's revelations of God strengthen our position?

3. God is revealed as the unaided Creator of the universe. How do you answer those who have been taught that evolution disproves the existence of God?

4. What comfort do you take from the fact that the fate of the nations and the activities of their rulers is in the hands of God? How should we pray, and what should we do?

5. God's word always comes to pass. What testimonies do you have to illustrate this truth? How do you respond when the promise appears not to be fulfilled?

_____

_____

_____

_____

6. Comparing John 4:20–24 with Isaiah 66:1–2, how would you describe the house of God? See also Ephesians 2:19–22.

_____

_____

_____

_____

7. What do you think it means to live in a 'zone of grace'? What is actually involved in having a humble and contrite heart? (See Personal Application below and Leader's Notes.)

_____

_____

_____

_____

Personal Application

It is sometimes alleged that God is not God enough, or not good enough to meet our human needs. He is either too small or too distant, or both. Yet God most high is also God most nigh. He is powerful enough to run the universe and close enough for us to experience His personal love and care.

The people who understand and experience this are those who, with humble and contrite hearts, respect God's Word (see Micah 6:8). Humility is often the missing element in our lives and its absence leaves us struggling between the poles of God's justice and His mercy. Once humble ourselves, the two poles become a tri-polar zone of grace, where we find the promised joy and peace that transforms resentment into rejoicing.

Seeing Jesus in the Scriptures

John's Gospel opens with the revelation that the eternal Word through whom the universe was made is also the One who became a human being named Jesus (see John 1:1–3,14). He who created the laws of the universe chose to become subject to those laws so we might know God for ourselves. We cannot reach God, but God has reached us. In Jesus, we see the justice, the mercy and the humility of God; it is pure grace reaching out and touching our lives with the Good Shepherd's love.

John could only marvel. '... we have heard ... we have seen with our eyes ... our hands have touched ... the Word of life' (1 John 1:1). May we similarly, through faith, worship the One and Only, who is at the Father's side.

Reality TV is a genre of TV programming that documents purportedly unscripted real-life situations, often starring unknown individuals rather than professional actors.

Idols – Pop Idol 2001 → The X Factor
Big Brother   Britain's Got Talent
criticisms of reality TV shows: they are intended to humiliate or exploit participants; that they make stars out of untalented people unworthy of fame, infamous figures, or both; and that they glamorize

WEEK 2 *Vulgarity.*

Tottering Idols

Opening Icebreaker

Draw up a 'name and shame' list of popular idols in our contemporary world. Write each one on a slip of paper. Gather these and 'ceremonially' destroy them – through the shredder, in the fireplace or simply screw them up and put them in the rubbish bin.

so called celebrities! Kardashians?

Bible Readings

- Isaiah 40:18–20 *Pg 831*
- Isaiah 41:7,21–24 *Pg 832/4*
- Isaiah 44:9–20 *Pg 837*
- Isaiah 45:20–21 *Pg 841*
- Isaiah 46:1–7 *Pg 842*

Key verse: 'All who make idols are nothing, and the things they treasure are worthless.' Isaiah 44:9

Focus: Keep yourselves from the superstitious folly of idols. Trust in the Lord, instead.

Opening Our Eyes

A man is a fool if he claims to be a god. How much more a fool if he claims that something he has manufactured with his own hands is a god. This is Isaiah's telling point. There is only one living God, the Creator and Redeemer of the entire universe, yet people worship idols of their own making and expect these objects to speak to them, to guide and protect them, to grant them a large family and big harvests. How crazy can you get?

In a scathing satire on idols and their worshippers, Isaiah sets out to demonstrate the powerlessness and futility of polytheism. With no regard for political correctness, he debunks the mumbo-jumbo with ice-cool logic. For a start, there are two kinds of idols, those the rich can afford, and those the poor can afford. So, it's a business, nothing more. The rich get the silver ones; the poor get the wood. There is no magic or mystery about idols; making them is just another job for the blacksmith or carpenter – four horseshoes, one latch, oh and a couple of idols! And when delivery takes place the idol has to be nailed down to stop it falling over. These 'gods' can't even stand on their own two feet!

Ah, but aren't the craftsmen inspired? Hardly. The blacksmith receives no supernatural aid. He grows just as thirsty making an idol as he does beating out a frying pan. The carpenter uses the same calculations and tools for the shaping and construction of an idol as he does for making a chair.

Surely then the materials are special, holy in some way? Observe, says Isaiah. Visit the forest. The woodsman fells a tree. Half of it he uses for firewood to cook a meal and to keep himself warm. The other half he carves into an idol and then he calls it his god! Has everyone switched their brains off? You are asking a block of wood to save you! What utter folly.

Can't you see that the power of the idol lies entirely
in the virtues that you attribute to it? It has no intrinsic
power or intelligence. Ask it to prophesy, to interpret
the past or the future. Get it to do anything! It can't, of
course. You are in a self-imposed superstitious bondage
to a thing. Instead of the idols carrying you, you have to
lug them around like so much baggage. Instead of them
upholding you, you have to make sure they don't fall
over in the wind. Don't waste your money, people.

Now, contrast this nonsense with the true and living God.
There is no likeness you can make to do justice to the
Lord of the forests, the Shepherd of the stars, the Founder
of the hills. Yet He speaks, He upholds, He guides, He
protects, He forgives sins, He redeems, He comforts and
sustains. He carries you; you don't have to carry Him. He
will keep you on your feet; there is no need for you to
prop Him up like some DIY tottering idol.

Idol worshippers, be they devotees of local gods or
national gods, will be embarrassed beyond measure
when their gods fail to act. The idols change their form
over the centuries, new religions spring up, old ones are
revamped, but it's always the same old folly. Turn from
such foolish and worthless practices and trust in the Lord,
for in the Lord is everlasting strength.

Discussion Starters

1. Why do you think people are superstitious? What is it that gives idols their appeal? In what ways does Jesus break their power?

2. How would you explain to a Hindu the difference between their worship of idols and your worship of the living God?

3. Isaiah wasn't politically correct. He told the truth. What can we learn from him when presenting our faith in a religiously pluralistic society?

4. How would you set about delivering someone from the power of idols if they have been heavily involved in the occult?

5. How do you explain to a Muslim that worshipping Jesus is neither idolatrous nor blasphemous?

_____

_____

_____

_____

6. What idols do you have or have you had in your life? What sort of things might you wish to dispose of? See Acts 19:18–20.

_____

_____

_____

_____

7. Where do you detect idolatry in our society? Is there any in the Church, and if so, what form does it take?

_____

_____

_____

_____

Personal Application

St Christopher, astral symbols, polytheistic faiths, icons and Buddhas, Wiccan symbols, New Age Yin Yang pendants – it's a very religious world. Add to this the plethora of charismatic personalities and performers, celebs and pop idols, and those electronic small objects of desire that we come to depend on, be it our iPhone or games consoles. Don't forget to include your investment portfolio, your car, your house. Idolatry, and the temptation to trust in things while paying lip-service to God, is rife. Temptations abound. John's last words in his first letter were never more apt: 'Dear children, keep yourselves from idols.'

It's not a question of what we could live without, but what we could live *happily and peacefully* without. Let our trust be in the Lord alone.

Seeing Jesus in the Scriptures

Jesus prophesied that in the last days there would be many false messiahs claiming to be God and demanding our worship. He warned us not to chase after them. He alone is the true revelation of the Father. Colossians 1:15 describes Him as the 'image of the invisible God', literally 'the icon'. But Jesus is no idol or substitute for the Father. He is, as Hebrews 1:3 puts it, 'the exact representation of his being'. Whoever has seen Him has seen the Father, for He is God incarnate. When we worship Him, we worship the only true and living God.

He is also the one Mediator between us and God (see 1 Tim. 2:5). To come to God via the virtues of anyone else, or anything else, is to fall into idolatry.

WEEK 3

The Nation that Failed

Opening Icebreaker

Design your own hypocrite. Invent a character, male or female, who epitomises hypocrisy. Try to think not only of their personal characteristics but illustrate these by some imagined actions on their part.

Backstabber
Two faced
False friend
recommend colleague for
Promotion then they take your job
and tell about you behind your
back

Bible Readings

* Isaiah 42:18–25   Pg 835
* Isaiah 57:1–13   Pg 854
* Isaiah 58:1–14   Pg 855
* Isaiah 59:1–18   Pg 856

Key verse: '… you have burdened me with your sins and wearied me with your offences.' Isaiah 43:24

Focus: Religious activity cannot compensate for decadent living and social injustice.

Opening Our Eyes

God chose the nation of Israel to bring blessing to every other nation on earth. They were not to be a superior race exercising the presumptions of power, but servants called uniquely to model a society that worshipped, loved and served the one true and living God. To this task they had willingly covenanted themselves at Sinai. God, for His part, promised to bless and protect them. He did so for the sake of His servant, Abraham, their patriarch from whose descendants one day would appear the Messiah, the Saviour of the world.

Instead of pursuing this high and noble calling, the nation became instead a byword for appalling decadence, corruption and injustice. Following the demise of the northern half of the kingdom, the southern half should have learned the price of disobedience. It did not. Sin followed sin and, through the prophet Isaiah, God charged this special 'holy' nation with a whole string of offences. Listen to the charge sheet: oppression of the poor, the unmitigated pursuit of greed, an economic system based on Fortune and Destiny, an utterly corrupt legal system, the murder of the innocent, the theft of their property. If that were not enough, the people were obsessed with their fertility rites – ceremonies that involved gross sexual promiscuity and sacrificing their children to pagan deities like Baal, Asherah and Molech. Idols and sacred shrines spattered the landscape, a sinister cult of the dead flourished in town and country alike. It led God to describe His people as the offspring of witches and prostitutes.

While all this was going on, the official state religion continued as though nothing were amiss. People still paid lip service to God; they even fasted and made offerings on the appropriate days. Unmitigated, wilful hypocrisy! God's word was crystal clear and heard often enough from the mouths of His prophets, but these corrupt people simply shut their ears and closed their eyes to the truth.

Despite centuries of faithlessness, God remained faithful. He blessed obedience, as He had promised, but the covenant was a double-edged sword. Patient as God was, the blade of judgment would inevitably strike if the decadence continued. Yet, even under the threat of punishment, God's offer of free forgiveness remained open, if only they would reform their ways. Indeed, when the sentence for their refusal of grace was served, God would sweep away their past misconduct and grant the nation a fresh start.

They didn't deserve it, but God had a reputation to keep! The nation may have been treacherous and rebellious from day one, but He was still intent on demonstrating that He was a God of justice and a God of grace. Babylon, the instrument of judgment, will fall when the job is done – according to God's justice – and God's people will be restored – according to God's grace.

In a theme launched early on in his prophetic ministry, Isaiah declares again God's non-interest in religion – however orthodox it may be – if it is not matched by ethical living. The only fasting that interests Him is the kind that results in giving up greed and injustice and 24/7 trading. God calls for government reform so that the needs of the poor are met. He wants equal employment legislation and a fair legal system for the impoverished. Sure, it will cost the wealthy, but that is the only sacrifice God will accept. Implement this and the nation will prosper from the blessings of obedience.

Discussion Starters

1. The failure of Israel is a challenge to the Church. What do you think are the issues where we need to repent so that we might be a good witness to the grace of God?

2. How do you think we can do justice both to loving God with all our hearts and ethically loving our neighbours? See James 1:27.

3. Sabbath observance is one of the Ten Commandments that must surely apply just as much as the others. Discuss the implications of this.

4. How would you call and practise an Isaiah 58 fast in your church?

5. Sexual promiscuity and child sacrifice were grievous features of Isaiah's society and the people's persistence in these sins brought judgment. What parallels do you see with our own society?

----

6. What message of grace would you offer those who know that their sinful lifestyle has brought suffering upon them?

----

7. How can we keep our ears and eyes open so that we do not grow deaf or blind to the will of God?

Personal Application

There are two kinds of hypocrisy: that which performs religious duties outwardly while hiding a heart far from God, and that which is devout before God but has no interest in the issues of justice and poverty. Neither are pleasing to the Lord.

To the first kind we say, God looks on the heart. What is done in secret sooner or later comes to the light. It is better to repent now and get it over with! To the second we say, remedy the sins of neglect. Romans 13:8–10 reminds us of Jesus' teaching that all the commands of God are fulfilled in just two – love God, love your neighbour (see Luke 10:27). Our neighbour is anyone we encounter in our journey through life, so be a good Samaritan at whatever level you can, politically, economically, personally.

Seeing Jesus in the Scriptures

Israel failed in its calling as the servant of the Lord. Jesus did not fail (see Isa. 42:4). He is the obedient One who did only what the Father was doing and as such was a faithful representation of God's perfect will. He is the faithful and true witness (see Rev. 3:14); He models for all of us what it means to serve the purpose of God. Even at the end of His life when He might have turned away from the cross, He cried, 'Not my will but yours be done.' Obedient even to death, He is now exalted to the right hand of the Father, demonstrating, as the true Israel, that God blesses those who keep His covenant.

WEEK 4

Here is My Servant

Opening Icebreaker

What does the death of Jesus mean to you and how has it changed your life? Have a few members of the group share a little of their own answers to these questions.

Bible Readings

- Isaiah 49:1–9 P 845
- Isaiah 52:13–53:12 P 850
- Isaiah 50:4–9 P 847
- Isaiah 61:1–3 P 859

Key verse: 'Here is my servant, whom I uphold, my chosen one in whom I delight; I will put my Spirit on him and he will bring justice to the nations.' Isaiah 42:1

Focus: Jesus of Nazareth is the promised Servant of the Lord, the Messiah, who came to save the world.

Opening Our Eyes

Israel's national failure to demonstrate and proclaim the truth about God sets the scene for Him to introduce His own true Servant. The life and the testimony that should have been theirs will be enshrined instead in one Man who is both the anointed King and the suffering Servant – the Messiah, no less!

Isaiah's remarkable prophecies, sometimes called 'Servant songs', find their long-awaited fulfilment in Jesus of Nazareth. The herald voice that announces the coming glory of the Lord is John the Baptist, whose ministry prepared the way for Jesus (see Isa. 40:3–5; Matt. 3:3; Luke 1:76).

This amazing Servant is chosen and anointed to establish justice across the whole world. He is no petty nationalistic rabble-rouser like Barabbas trying to shake off the Roman yoke, but a world leader; the Servant is a covenant to the people and a light for the Gentiles. He will set captives free irrespective of their nationality and will bring salvation to the ends of the earth (see Isa. 49:6).

It will be a difficult task. The Servant speaks as the sword of the Spirit. He is Himself the revelation of God's glory. Yet His efforts to restore the spiritual life of Israel will see small reward in His lifetime. Not that it will stop Him; the Spirit of God is upon Him to fulfil a mandate of liberation for all who are oppressed, whatever form that oppression takes (see Isa. 61:1–3; Luke 4:18–21). Jesus will not fail or be discouraged until righteousness and praise replace oppression and misery in every nation on earth. The Servant is no softy but a mighty warrior who judges wickedness and who will rule the nations with an iron rod (see Rev. 5:5; 19:11–16). As King of kings and Lord of lords He will command the respect of the world's leaders.

So, what of the character of this mighty Servant? Here is the astonishing part that causes many to stumble in confusion. This world ruler is a humble man who listens daily to God. He comes from a despised northern town, the suspect child of a peasant woman, a working-class man who people wouldn't consider twice. Rather than resisting, He surrenders Himself to His persecutors, trusting that God will vindicate Him (see Isa. 50:4–9). This self-humbling, which the apostle Paul expressed so eloquently in Philippians 2:5–11, finds its fullest expression in the best known of the 'Servant songs', the suffering Servant of Isaiah 52:13–53:12.

The hope of Israel, the Saviour of the world, is despised and rejected by those He came to save. He is beaten to a pulp and His mangled body is nailed to a tree to die. The sight is fearsome, obscene and repulsive. What terrible sin has He committed? Why is He so accursed? Isaiah tells us. This Man bears in His own body our sicknesses and our sins. He is nailed up and run through for our transgressions, crushed for our iniquities, flogged to shreds for our healing. The Servant is suffering in our place, the willing Lamb of God, dying for us wilful, wandering sheep. Killed in the prime of life, unmarried and childless, He is buried like a common criminal.

Amazingly, it is no mistake; the Servant is fulfilling God's will. Dying, He will rise again and produce many spiritual offspring. He will live for ever and on the merits of His sacrifice all who come to know Him will be made right with God.

Discussion Starters

1. How would you explain to a Jewish friend that Jesus of Nazareth is the fulfilment of the Servant promises in Matthew 12:18–21? Why was Jesus cursed and yet still the Promised One?

2. The doctrine of substitutionary atonement (Jesus bearing our sins on the cross to free us from the guilt, penalty and power of sin) has been attacked as immoral in recent years. What does it mean and why is this such an important truth in your life?

3. We are described as wandering sheep. How do you explain what this means to your not-yet-believing acquaintances?

4. Jesus died for both our sicknesses and our sins. Why is it that we can be sure that all our sins are forgiven through faith in Him, but not necessarily all our sicknesses are healed in this life?

_____

_____

_____

_____

5. Jesus' Nazareth manifesto promised political, economic, social, physical and spiritual release. How do we offer this today?

_____

_____

_____

_____

6. The suffering Servant is also the warrior bringing judgment. The first coming leads to the second coming. What bearing does this have on how we communicate the gospel? How do we prepare the way of the Lord today?

_____

_____

_____

_____

7. The gospel was to go first to the Jews and then to all nations. How involved are you in the Church's missionary vision? Is there anything more you should be doing?

_____

_____

_____

_____

Personal Application

The Servant, Jesus, modelled for us what it means to live a life pleasing to God. Jesus was both humble and determined, gracious but strong, compassionate but uncompromising. How do we match up? The world still needs to see and to hear Jesus. The only possible way most people can do so is through the testimony of our lives and the words of our mouths.

This would be daunting if we were simply trying to mimic Jesus, but He has granted us the gift of the Holy Spirit to sanctify and empower us (see Gal. 5:22–23; Acts 1:8). By daily submitting ourselves to the Spirit of God, as Jesus did, we shall become good examples of what it means to be the Lord's servants.

Seeing Jesus in the Scriptures

The substitutionary atonement of Christ changed salvation history for all time. Until that point, regulatory animal sacrifices had been offered to take away sins. Jesus initiated a new covenant that rendered these obsolete because it is based upon the once-and-for-all offering of His own blood. Because He lives and intercedes for us, this offering has permanent efficacy, ensuring that we are always accepted before the Father (see Heb. 8:12). There is no condemnation because the price of our redemption has been paid in full.

Jesus has a lot of children as a result of His obedience. He is the Seed that fell into the ground and died but which now brings forth much fruit. As one of His children you have the inestimable privilege of being a joint-heir of glory with Christ.

WEEK 5

Cyrus, the Anointed Pagan

Opening Icebreaker

Share brief stories about when God has helped you through the most unlikely and, possibly, quite scary people.

Bible Readings

- Isaiah 41:1–4,25–29
- Isaiah 44:24–45:17
- Isaiah 46:1–47:15

- 1 Timothy 2:1–4
- Romans 13:1–7
- Revelation 5:9–10

Key verse: 'I make known the end from the beginning, from ancient times, what is still to come. I say: My purpose will stand, and I will do all that I please.' Isaiah 46:10

Focus: The Sovereign Lord raises up and puts down kingdoms for the sake of His own saving purposes.

Opening Our Eyes

There is only one thing God cannot do. He cannot be false to Himself. Beyond that, He can do anything He wants and never feels obliged to explain or to be ashamed of His actions! To us, His works will sometimes appear outrageous. As a case in point, the Lord God declares that He is going to anoint a pagan Iranian king named Cyrus to restore His people to their homeland. Impossible? Theologically unsound? Offensive?

Graciously, on this occasion, God invites the cynics to a public hearing to declare that He is the one, nobody else, who will raise up Cyrus, 'the one from the east', to serve His purposes – in this case to conquer Babylon. Cyrus will invade from a northerly direction, crushing this mighty empire out of existence. Such an upheaval will seem very threatening to the exiles living in Babylon, but they should not fear. This is the Lord's doing, and to prepare them He has let His people know well in advance. In spite of the dire prognostications of false prophets and fortune tellers, Jerusalem will be rebuilt. Cyrus, though he doesn't know it, will become the shepherd of God's people and order the reconstruction.

Indeed, Cyrus is anointed by God to change the entire balance of power and to institute a new world order in the Middle East. Although Cyrus neither knows nor acknowledges God, he will prove to be the instrument through which the world discovers that there is no other God. Furthermore, God is not just a private talisman, nor a mere national deity; He exercises sovereign power over the political affairs of all nations.

Lest Cyrus should wish to quarrel with this political analysis, the Lord reminds him that he is just a piece of broken pottery with no more rights to protest than the clay has to argue with the potter, or babies to challenge their parents about their conception and birth. Does anyone else wish to take offence over the idea of God using a pagan idol worshipper? God reminds His people that He is the Creator of the universe and the One who marshals the stars – a pert reminder to astrology-obsessed Babylon and Persia that the stars are not gods! Like it or not, God in His righteousness will use this king and order the nations to restore His saving purpose in the earth – for out of Zion will come the Redeemer!

As for that Babylonian witch-queen, she is finished. In her arrogance and imperial ambition she abused God's people, little thinking that she should have shown mercy because she was the instrument of God's judicial processes. Secure in her wanton pride she thought to last for ever. But no longer! She will lose everything and in a single day be reduced to the level of a serf. Her magic will fail, however many spells she weaves, and however many stargazers she employs.

What of the gods of Babylon? Do they not have any power? After all, they surely enabled the Babylonians to overrun Jerusalem. Watch this space, says the Lord. The Babylonian idols will not save them from His servant, Cyrus. Whereas He carries His people, Bel and Nebo must be loaded up onto oxen to be moved around. What irony! They can't even walk! So listen up, you doubters! There is only one God and His purposes are timeless. When He says that salvation will come, then it surely will!

Discussion Starters

1. What do you consider are the opportunities and limits of Christian involvement in politics?

_____

_____

_____

_____

2. What guidelines do you think we should follow in praying for the governments of the world?

_____

_____

_____

_____

3. What comfort can you offer to those living under oppressive regimes in the light of Christ's rule over the nations?

_____

_____

_____

_____

4. Sadly, many MPs testify that the most personally offensive letters they receive come from professing Christians. How do you think we should deal with our political leaders, locally, nationally or internationally, when we have a valid point to make?

_____

_____

_____

_____

5. There are many false prophets and pundits today, some of them 'occult' and some not. What identifies them and how do you respond to their prognostications?

_____

_____

_____

_____

6. God works politically so that all nations may hear the gospel and that people may come to know Him. How should this affect our missionary praying?

_____

_____

_____

_____

7. The Church is called to engage in spiritual warfare. In the light of Christ's rule over the rulers of this world, how should we be using the sword of the Spirit?

_____

_____

_____

_____

Personal Application

We must avoid dividing our lives into sacred and secular compartments. Pietism that ignores politics is unbiblical, as is politics that has no time for devotion to God. We are commanded to pray for our governments (see 1 Tim. 2:1–4); to exercise our citizenship in the cause of justice (see Acts 16:37–40); to respect the principle of just government (see Rom. 13:1–7); to resist the incursions of evil when it comes to the persecution of our faith (see 1 Pet. 4:14–16).

At the heart of this must be a desire to see Christ's kingdom come through the proclamation of the gospel. No lesser motive will do; no greater one is possible. Let's engage with social issues and political opportunities, and not detach ourselves from them.

Seeing Jesus in the Scriptures

Jesus is the King of kings and the Lord of lords. He is the President of presidents and the Governor of governors. Whatever power men might suppose they have, their power is delegated to them by Christ. He is seated at God's right hand and from this commanding position looses the seals of the scroll that determines human history (see Rev. 5:9–10). It may not always be comfortable, but the hands that loose the seals are nail-pierced. Our loving Saviour reigns!

His sacrificial love sets the standard for world leaders and they will be judged by the degree to which they, as responsible agents, governed for the benefit of their peoples. In particular, Jesus is concerned about justice and integrity and the protection of the vulnerable and the freedom of people to worship Him.

WEEK 6

The Restored Remnant

Opening Icebreaker

Start your meeting with some party food and cheerful music. Share simple stories about occasions when your sadness has turned into exuberant joy.

Bible Readings

- Isaiah 40:1–11
- Isaiah 41:11–20
- Isaiah 43:1–7

- Isaiah 49:8–26
- Isaiah 52:1–12
- Daniel 9:1–19

Key verse: 'The ransomed of the LORD will return. They will enter Zion with singing; everlasting joy will crown their heads. Gladness and joy will overtake them, and sorrow and sighing will flee away.' Isaiah 51:11

Focus: God's saving purposes are vested in those who remain faithful to Him.

Opening Our Eyes

In 586BC, just as Isaiah prophesied it would, Jerusalem fell to the Babylonians. All its prominent citizens – the government and civil service, the military leaders, the educators, the medics, the business leaders – were deported. With no infrastructure, national identity collapsed. Foreign peasants were imported and intermingled with the remaining Jewish peasantry. On them fell the fiscal burden of producing food and goods for the benefit of their Babylonian overlords. To all intents and purposes, the great theocratic experiment was at an end; the nation of Israel was finished. God had lost the battle; He had failed to produce a holy nation.

Or had He? From the start of his prophetic ministry Isaiah had spoken about a holy remnant. This group of people consisted of those who remained faithful to God and who refused to worship idols. In them God had invested His saving purposes for the nation and for the world. They carried the spiritual seed in their genes – and they took it all the way to Babylon, and back again. They were the holy stump (see Isa. 6:13) that one day would regrow even though it had been cut down and burned. The righteous suffering along with the wicked might seem unfair, but, like Isaiah himself, the remnant willingly, albeit painfully, identified with the sins of the people and accepted the judgment when it came. So, they experienced the destruction of their capital city and its Temple; they went into captivity, and in captivity they underwent the journey of repentance that would pave the way for the restoration and return. No one expressed this better than the exiled prophet Daniel (see Dan. 9:1–19).

In spite of the difficulties, God never forgot this faithful remnant and it is to them that He addresses His opening words of comfort. The 'worm' – powerless, despised, trampled upon – will be transformed into a sharp threshing machine that will thrash through the difficulties and return to Zion. The journey might take them through fire and water, but the remnant will not be harmed, for their Creator is also their Protector and Redeemer. Wherever they have been scattered they will return and, incredibly, their overlords will foot the bill!

This will happen because God is a covenant God who always, at the right time, fulfils His word. However discouraged His people might feel, however cynical some might be, however lacking in resources and strength, God will do it. All-powerful Babylon will fall overnight and a new regime will arise that will liberate God's people. Indeed, this will be nothing less than a second Exodus, a return to the promised land. This time, however, the wilderness will be transformed into a place of fruitfulness, making the journey direct and bearable. The Lord's ransomed ones will return to Zion, singing and rejoicing, carrying the money that their new overlords will supply for rebuilding the city and its temple. Such is God's grace towards His faithful people. Rebuke followed by repentance always leads to revival and restoration.

Small in number they might be, but they would soon multiply. Israel was like an abandoned wife, childless and destitute, but the Lord will gather her to Himself. He will be her husband, and the union will produce a multitude of children. This being the case, they should think big and prepare for growth. Their little nation will grow and become famous throughout the world – the source of light and hope to the entire human race.

Discussion Starters

1. Those who bring good news have 'beautiful feet'. How should this affect our attitude towards those who preach the gospel and towards our own witnessing for Christ?

2. How would you explain in comprehensible terms to the average decent unbeliever that they need redeeming from the hand of the enemy?

3. How might you use the words of Isaiah 54 to comfort an abandoned or widowed wife? What comfort can we all draw from this passage?

4. What parallels, if any, do you see between the restoration of Israel under Cyrus and the re-establishing of the nation of Israel following the Nazi Holocaust?

5. What are the conditions for backsliders to return to the Lord and what encouragement can you offer them from Isaiah's words?

_____

_____

_____

_____

6. What do you think it means for God's people to be a 'threshing-sledge, new and sharp, with many teeth'? What are these mountains and hills in our lives and in our society?

_____

_____

_____

_____

7. God's restored people will welcome foreigners and eunuchs, those previously excluded from the Temple. Jesus said that His house would be a house of prayer for all nations. What implications does this have for the Church today and for your church in particular?

_____

_____

_____

_____

Personal Application

God our Saviour is faithful to His covenant word, and believers are members of the new covenant ratified by Christ's blood. The restoration of God's people points to the release of all those born in captivity to the world, the flesh and the devil. They have been set free by the power of this new covenant. Jesus paid the ransom price for our release so that we might join the Lord's redeemed. We have come to Zion (see Heb. 12:22–24). Little wonder that we celebrate our salvation!

Are you living in the good of your redemption or have you fallen back? God loves to restore the penitent. Individuals and churches alike can experience spiritual revival and know again the joy of salvation.

Seeing Jesus in the Scriptures

John the Baptist's prophetic call, first voiced by Isaiah, marks him as the herald who brings the good news of Christ's advent. John identified Jesus of Nazareth as the One fulfilling his words. The restoration of Israel to their homeland becomes then a remarkable metaphor for the work of the gospel. Jesus is our anointed Saviour, rescuing us from our bondage to the law of sin and death. He is the One who grants us new life and who turns our mourning into dancing. He is our good Shepherd leading us through the wilderness, transforming our barrenness into fruitfulness. He is the Bridegroom to the Bride, comforting and restoring, beautifying us and making our lives fruitful. He is the coming King who will one day gather us all to Himself. Praise His name!

WEEK 7

The Worldwide Church

Opening Icebreaker

Using sheets of paper, create 'barricades' between one of your number and everyone else. Write on each sheet of paper one of the barriers between human beings, especially between Jew and Gentile. See how many you can think of. Cancel these one by one by coming up with different ways that Jesus renders these barriers obsolete. Then you can have a hug!

Bible Readings

- Isaiah 42:1–10
- Isaiah 45:22–25
- Isaiah 54:1–5
- Isaiah 55:1–5
- Isaiah 59:19–60:5
- Hebrews 12:22–24

Key verse: 'Turn to me and be saved, all you ends of the earth; for I am God, and there is no other.' Isaiah 45:22

Focus: The faithful remnant was destined to birth a church without boundaries through a gospel that excludes no one.

Opening Our Eyes

Quite apart from Ishmael, Abraham produced two lines of descent – one biological, and one spiritual; one of race, and one of grace. Belonging to the one did not automatically mean you belonged to the other. The grace line was entered by faith and though many Israelites did believe, many others did not. Occasionally, Gentiles, like Rahab, might enter the faith line, too. This faith line formed the remnant – those looking for the coming of Christ and living already by faith in the new covenant (see John 8:56–58; Heb. 11:13; 1 Pet. 1:10–12).

Isaiah foresaw that the rare instances of regenerate Gentiles would one day become normal and universal. Through faith in Christ, vast numbers of Gentiles would be grafted into the spiritual rootstock of Abraham. The children of the restored bride – the remnant – refers not just to the physical repopulating of Palestine after the exile but will include a dramatic spiritual enlargement of Israel. This 'desolate woman' will have more children than she could ever imagine! Those of Jewish descent and those of Gentile descent who together enter the faith line of Abraham through Christ will constitute a vastly extended family, the Church of the firstborn.

To implement this amazing prophecy, God will institute a new covenant where racial, religious and cultural background will no longer matter; nor will worship be restricted to particular holy places (see John 4:21). God's glory will circle the globe (see Gal. 3:26–29; 6:15–16; Isa. 59:19; 66:1–2). No one is excluded from the new deal! Foreigners are welcome, the fruitless and barren, all who love the Lord and honour His Sabbath rest may find joy in His house of prayer. Salvation is offered to the whole world!

Should natural Israel resent this? On the contrary, far from losing their special status they should rejoice that Christ has fulfilled their servant calling. This new covenant is issued through one of their own. From Christ's teaching and passion, located in earthly Palestine, but originating in heavenly Zion, the law of God – the saving gospel of grace – goes to all nations. What an honour! The Christian gospel is not an enemy of Judaism but its fulfilment. Emanating from the heart of Judaism the gospel is taken by Jews, in accord with Isaiah's prophesy, to Jerusalem, Judea, Samaria and the ends of the earth. Peace is offered equally to those who are near and to those who are far off (see Eph. 2:14–18).

Be proud, O Israel, that the Lord has done this. Jesus is your glory! Your Messiah will make you famous, your scriptures are the ones they will read, your city the one of which they will sing. For earthly Jerusalem is the metaphor for heavenly Jerusalem, our true mother (see Gal. 4:26–27; Isa. 60:19–20; Rev. 21:1–2). There is no earthly house that can contain the Lord of heaven and earth, but He will dwell with all who possess humble and contrite hearts. Mount Zion is accessible to anyone, anywhere (see Heb. 12:22–24).

This new Jerusalem, free from ageing and aggression, will one day descend from heaven and God will create a new heavens and a new earth (see Isa. 65:17). Thebes, Nineveh and Babylon are history; the new Jerusalem is tomorrow! Meanwhile, the offspring of Christ and the heavenly woman, Jerusalem, continue to multiply across the world, fulfilling God's promise to Abraham, '... all peoples on earth will be blessed through you' (Gen. 12:3). From a faithful remnant has emerged the glorious worldwide Church.

Discussion Starters

1. How would you explain to a Jewish friend that rather than despising Jesus he should be proud of Him and accept Him as his Messiah?

_____

_____

_____

_____

2. Some people believe that the Church replaced Israel as the people of God. Others believe that the Church is insignificant compared to a proposed future national dominance of the state of Israel. From our study of the enlarged remnant, what do you think? How do you address those who hold such divergent views?

_____

_____

_____

_____

3. In the light of the universal appeal of the gospel, what extra steps might your church take to ensure that the message of salvation reaches all nations and people groups?

_____

_____

_____

_____

4. What are the implications of Jesus' words to the woman of Samaria about there being no geographic centre to the worship of God (see John 4:21; Isa. 66:1–2)?

_____

_____

_____

_____

5. What do you understand by Jesus, the Servant of the Lord, being a light to the Gentiles?

_____

_____

_____

_____

6. In the light of Isaiah's prophecy, what can we learn from Paul's teaching on the peace that Christ has accomplished (see Eph. 2:11–17)?

_____

_____

_____

_____

7. Earthly Jerusalem is a dim and now distorted metaphor for Jerusalem above. As those who have come to the heavenly Mount Zion (see Heb. 12:22–24) what implications does this have for your life and walk with God?

_____

_____

_____

_____

Personal Application

How big is your vision? It is very easy to have a narrow, pietistic vision that affects only our lives and those of our immediate family and friends. Does God really only work through our church or movement, or denominational family? He is the God of the whole earth! The gospel message is unrestricted. Wherever the Spirit of God may go, the gospel may go. The Church is not the remnant desperately holding on until the Lord comes. God has purposed that His Son's name shall be known in all nations. So, will you play your part in spreading this unstoppable gospel wherever you can?

Seeing Jesus in the Scriptures

Abraham rejoiced to see the coming of Christ. He was justified by faith in the Promised One and through his seed all the nations of the earth will be blessed. God commissioned His Servant Jesus not only to bring salvation to natural Israel but also to be a light to the Gentiles. All people will see His glory and His praise will be sung around the world. Every knee will bow to Him and His new covenant law will illuminate the world's governments. All peoples and all races are welcome in His glorious kingdom.

From this insignificant little nation, from an unknown peasant woman in a backwater town, has emerged One who is honoured in every nation on earth, just as the Lord promised through Isaiah. The word of the Lord never fails to accomplish His purpose. We may not yet see everything under His feet, but we see Jesus, crowned with glory and honour!

Leader's Notes

It makes good sense in approaching part two of Isaiah's great prophecy if you also study part one in this series. Although there is a continuity gap between the two halves, we hold that the Isaiah who prophesied the defeat of Assyria in his own time also prophesied, beyond his lifetime, the Babylonian invasion, the exile and the restoration of God's people. Furthermore, Isaiah also prophesied the coming of Christ and the worldwide spread of the gospel through the Church.

Read the Introduction to your group and, if possible, show them a map of the Babylonian and Persian empires of the period. If you have access to a Bible timeline it will help your group to understand the context better. Isaiah's poetic prophecy is best treated as a mighty operatic performance. With this in mind we shall group the material under the headings of the main players in the drama rather than treating the prophecies sequentially. Encourage your group members to read a chapter a day during the course of this series of studies.

Week 1: There is Only One God

The Opening Icebreaker is best done by using a whiteboard or equivalent to write up the characteristics of your invented god as people bring them. Keep this visible throughout this session so that you can compare what you have written with what the Scriptures reveal. You may want to add to it as you go. Each week ask different people to do the readings, then read aloud the Opening Our Eyes section.

This week's session evokes praise almost from the beginning. God is just awesome! Be enthusiastic about these great foundational truths. If we can't get our understanding of God right then we shall go astray on everything else. These powerful words lift our eyes to the greatness of God – and they also put us humans in context. We are like summer grass. Our world leaders are short-lived and have little control over their destiny. Our efforts at religion are vain and pathetic in the light of the reality of God. Yet our great Creator is our loving Shepherd and He delights to dwell with all those who seek Him with a contrite heart. This truly is amazing grace!

The first three Discussion Starters are designed to help us relate our faith to our contemporary society and its challenge to our beliefs. Use the questions as an exercise to train group members to articulate their faith in the marketplace of life. Regarding Discussion Starter 3, don't get sidetracked by lengthy discussions over evolution; however God did it, *God* did it, and it was no accident or random event.

Discussion Starter 4 reminds us that we must not be detached from world politics. Our prayers make a difference, as do our actions!

Read the Personal Application before addressing the last three Discussion Starters. Keep the stories brief when discussing 5. The second part of the question helps us remember that not everything is a success story. Heaven's silence can be very frustrating but it is also an opportunity for spiritual growth. Discussion Starter 7 reminds us that humility is the key that releases us into the zone of grace. Draw a line, marking the two ends justice and mercy, respectively. Then, with a third point underneath, marked humility, create an inverted triangle. In the middle of the triangle write the word grace.

Read the Seeing Jesus section and use Discussion Starter 6 to make the point that Jesus is the living Temple, present with us by His Spirit wherever we are. With this in mind, you may well like to end this session with a time of worship.

Week 2: Tottering Idols

The Opening Icebreaker is designed to help us realise that idol worship is not just an ancient or overseas phenomenon. Your list might include Hindu and Buddhist idols, occult idols, celebrities, rock stars, consumer goods, 'Christian' idols.

Satire and irony have a healthy and noble history in Christian apologetics as a way of debunking popular misconceptions about the faith and exposing the folly of godless behaviour. Isaiah is not afraid to use them to good effect. Idolators have thrown their brains away, he declares. When men cease to believe in God they will believe in anything. Idol making is just another commercial enterprise. The mystique is of our own making. Self-delusion! Don't confuse the power of artistic representation with the power of deity. A tree is a tree; that's it. Your idols can't even walk; you have to carry the worthless things. How degrading! Idol worship is just so very foolish. Pious respect is an inappropriate response to such delusional practices.

Draw the stark contrast between this and the worship of the true and living God. There is no image that we can or should make of Him. He is the Lord of the forests, stars and hills that idolators worship. He is the Creator – and He acts. He answers prayer. He intervenes in the affairs of men and He controls the destiny of nations.

Idolatry is a reality in our society and Jesus' missionary mandate requires us to teach people to turn from idols and serve the living God (see 1 Thess. 1:9). The Discussion Starters are designed to help us do just that.

Using Discussion Starter 1, explain that the root of superstition is insecurity and fear. Find some examples. The perfect love of God drives out fear.

Discussion Starter 2 obliges us to face the complexity of Hinduism which often combines idol worship along with a belief in a supreme deity. Isaiah addressed just such a situation in Israel.

We should not be offensive but wise and sensitive in our witness, but there's no avoiding the fact that the truth will offend. Using Discussion Starter 3, come up with practical suggestions about how to speak about our convictions in our work and leisure times.

Idol worshippers must call upon the Lord to be saved; they must renounce all other gods and objects of worship and dispose of them. Some form of exorcism by mature Christians may well be required. Use Discussion Starter 4 to explore how practically this process may be undertaken.

Read the Seeing Jesus section as preparation for Discussion Starter 5. Islam teaches that representational art and religious images are idolatrous. To call Jesus the image of God is to them blasphemous, as is worshipping the Son of God. To us it is grace; God in mercy visiting us, coming down so that we might be raised up. Denying this fundamental truth reveals the spirit of antichrist – see 1 John 4:2–3. We do not believe in three Gods but in one God who expresses Himself in three Persons, so we are not idolators.

Read the Personal Application section before tackling

Discussion Starters 6 and 7. Encourage people to be honest at this point. What are the secret idols in our own lives, those superstitions of the mind that block our trust in the Lord, those items we fearfully cling to? Where, too, do we find idolatry in our secular culture? Finally, are there traditions of men in our churches, or even objects of veneration, that have become idolatrous? End this session with prayer for any in your group who need help with these issues.

Week 3: The Nation that Failed

This Opening Icebreaker should be tackled in a light-hearted manner, but it has a serious point. Hypocrisy is sin.

The Opening Our Eyes section focuses on the servant nature of God's calling for Israel to prepare the way for the Messiah. To do so required that they keep the faith of Abraham and worship only one God, obeying His commandments. Instead, Israel tried to mix it. Embracing the worship of the Canaanite fertility pantheon with its death cult, sexual promiscuity and child abuse, they lost the moral foundation for their nation. Government corruption, exploitation of the poor, and religious hypocrisy ousted righteous living. Yet the state religion of Moses continued in outward form – an arrogant expression of national pride.

It is said that the mills of God grind slowly. Patiently, faithfully, He still blessed His ungrateful people, warning them of inevitable judgment if they continued on their decadent path, but at the same time offering unconditional forgiveness if they would amend their ways. Justice and mercy go hand in hand. Combined with humility on our part they release grace. But God's people would have none of it and judgment proved the only way to bring about repentance.

Isaiah stresses repeatedly that God has no interest in mere religion. Worship must be combined with ethical living, and government policy must encourage and protect it. The will of God has not changed (see Micah 6:8). Discussion Starter 1 challenges us to think seriously about the quality and integrity of our lives. This inevitably demands that we show our love for God by our love for our neighbours. In 1 John 3:17–18 it is made plain that this must be practical. Use Discussion Starter 2 to come up with ways of making this a reality.

Jesus made it clear that the Sabbath was a mercy instituted by God for the protection of workers. Abolishing it for the sake of trade is offensive to Him and in time brings financial collapse. Use Discussion Starter 3 to discuss the extent to which this has a bearing on our personal and national economies.

An Isaiah 58 fast is one that puts to rights economic and social injustice. Discussion Starter 4 invites us to come up with some practical ideas for raising awareness and taking action. We may not be able to solve all the problems but if enough people do a little we might just change the world!

It isn't too difficult to see parallels between Israel's society and our own concerning sexual promiscuity and child sacrifice. The one difference is that we do not indulge in these vices for religious reasons. Discussion Starter 5 should involve talking about to what extent God's judgment on His chosen servant could apply to secular nations. Do we ignore people's behaviour knowing that only the gospel will really change them, or do we warn of the wrath to come and seek to legislate for morality? Or both?

Jesus came for the sick, the outcasts, the unclean, not for those who needed no help (see Mark 2:17). Discussion Starter 6 invites us not to theorise about the gospel but to ask to what extent our church is reaching those that Jesus came to reach.

Read the Personal Application section at this point then go on to Discussion Starter 7. Israel had grown numb to the voice of the prophets. How do we avoid drifting into callous hypocrisy without even realising it? How can we help one another to keep alert to God's voice?

End this session with the Seeing Jesus section. The nation failed dismally but God had His true Servant prepared.

Week 4: Here is My Servant

This Opening Icebreaker is a simple opportunity for a few personal testimonies. Maybe keep control of the more long-winded by setting a timer of some kind!

This session takes us to the heart of Isaiah's message and arguably, in Isaiah 53, to the most profound prophecy in the Bible. The so-called Servant Songs of Isaiah demonstrate that hidden within the corruption of the nation, God was preserving a line of faith that would culminate in the advent of the Messiah. The nation's servant destiny is fulfilled in one Man and the New Testament writers unequivocally identify Jesus of Nazareth as that Man.

We discover that the Messiah has a global ministry; His task is not to make Israel top of the pile as the nationalists understood it, but to bring moral and spiritual light and salvation to all nations. Indeed, His message will receive a poor hearing in His lifetime, but that will not deter Him. God's Spirit impels and empowers the Messiah to liberate the oppressed, whatever form that oppression takes, be it spiritual, moral, personal, economic or political. He will govern the nations in righteousness.

Here is the twist that you need to emphasise. This mighty Deliverer comes in humility, modelling in Himself the humility required of His followers, and living out the divine pattern of dying being the only way to true life. The culmination is recorded prophetically in Isaiah 53. The Messiah allows Himself to be destroyed by a combination of religious hypocrisy, mob violence, political totalitarianism, sadistic soldiery, moral cowardice and satanic hatred. Astonishingly, this is the will of God – Jesus is bearing our sins and sicknesses; He is the divine Substitute, and from His death will come life for the world.

Discussion Starters 1 and 2 enable us to deal with the Jewish stumbling block. How can a man hanged on a tree, by definition cursed by God (see Deut. 21:23), possibly be the Messiah? The answer lies in substitutionary atonement – Christ died in our place and in that one act dealt with the guilt, penalty and power of sin. It's not just a Jewish problem. Some church leaders have questioned the moral validity of Jesus being punished by God. Yet God is not a sadist. His love implies justice and justice implies punishment for sin. Jesus willingly undertook to bear the punishment for our sins. Read the Seeing Jesus section at this point to help people grasp this.

In using Discussion Starter 3, help people understand the imagery by illustrating how we all like our own way even when it damages us. Remind your group that lost sheep have a Good Shepherd who is out looking for them and calling their name. That's what our non-Christian acquaintances need to hear!

Discussion Starter 4 is a big question and you will not answer it fully in this session. Emphasise the key points, i.e. God is a healer; faith in Jesus will always result in healing but not necessarily in this life; the body is not yet redeemed but one day will be; our love and faithfulness to the Lord whatever our circumstances is part of our testimony.

Discussion Starters 5, 6 and 7 focus our attention on our missionary calling. They emphasise the holistic nature of the gospel, the urgency with which we are to proclaim it, and the practical action that we should take. Seek to inspire your group and pray together that the Holy Spirit will empower, equip and enable us to fulfil the servant task in our generation.

Week 5: Cyrus, the Anointed Pagan

Angels come in many guises. Sometimes they are in people who look more likely to mug us than assist us. An atheist might well be our good Samaritan. Share some examples together to remind us that God can use anybody for His will, even Baalam's ass!

The choice of an Iranian king named Cyrus, before he was born, is a startling example of God's predestination and a reminder that He knows the beginning from the end. Not only will Babylon invade Judah, destroy Jerusalem and take its people into a seventy-year captivity, but in turn Iran will invade Babylon and restore God's people to their homeland. Even more unlikely, the king of Iran, Cyrus, will be an absolute pagan who neither knows nor acknowledges God. So much for our tidy theology!

God has no need to justify His actions but in this case He invites His critics to a public hearing to let everyone know in advance that these great political events are His doing. There is only one God and no one should doubt His sovereignty over the affairs of man. Cyrus may think he has despotic power but in reality he is just a piece of clay in the Potter's hands. As for the other so-called gods, they are nothing. The stars are not deities; they are created matter organised by the living God.

Babylon was the centre of a great occult empire – a witch-queen who assumed that she had conquered God's people by her own strength and superior gods. Isaiah prophesies that she will fall to the will of God and her gods will prove useless. That's precisely what happened.

The Discussion Starters are intended to release us from our petty personal concerns and to focus our attention on the kingdom of God. Biblical Christians cannot withdraw from politics and concentrate only on personal piety. Use Discussion Starters 1 and 2 to consider how we get involved with the structures of our society and how we should pray. Don't let this descend into arguments about party politics. Christians must live above the categories and prejudices of men. Do talk about local involvement in areas such as school government. Read the Personal Application section for some biblical principles. Discussion Starter 3 reminds us that many of God's people suffer persecution for their faith. Suggest that we not only pray but we write, we petition, we demonstrate for their freedom. Discussion Starter 4 makes the sad point that some Christians are personally offensive when they communicate with their politicians. This is not only wrong but ineffective. Come up with some positive guidelines. Isaiah prophesied the truth. He did so in the face of the false prophets. Discussion Starter 5 provides an opportunity to consider how we discern the true from the false. Use contemporary examples of false prophecy to illustrate, e.g. the Millennium Bug, the nuclear holocaust, bird flu. What about global warming and the return of Christ? What is our basis for assessing prophecy (see 2 Pet. 1:16–21)?

Read the Seeing Jesus section, then address Discussion Starters 6 and 7. God raised up Cyrus as a step towards His purpose of appointing His Son Jesus as King of kings and Lord of lords. That has come to pass but the world needs to be told. It is our political task to announce the good news of the lordship of Christ to all nations. To that end we must pray persistently and in faith. We must wield the sword of the Spirit knowing that the truth will triumph. Encourage your group to do just that.

Week 6: The Restored Remnant

The food for the Opening Icebreaker could be a prearranged meal or a finger buffet or just nibbles. Choose happy music that isn't religious. The stories could range from finding a lost child to a dramatically reduced bill, from the restoration of a broken relationship to good news from the hospital.

Help your group imagine a nation like our own with no doctors or nurses, no employers, local council services, police force, teachers or armed forces. Everyone who runs society has been deported or killed. Those who are left have to pay most of their earnings to a country that has obliterated every building of note in your capital city and has wiped out most of the population. You are told it's the judgment of God, and you are so depressed that you agree. Or you may feel that you backed the wrong god and lost.

For all that, you might be one of the faithful who heeded Isaiah's words and lived according to God's will. It dawns on you that you have both a genetic destiny and a spiritual one. You are a member of the holy remnant. God will not forget you or your descendants. In seventy years' time a miracle will occur and the remnant will return to rebuild their land. Amazingly, your new colonial power will pay for it.

In 539BC, Cyrus conquered Babylon and in a few short years the exiles began to return to their homeland. It was a second Exodus and this time those who returned were true to the covenant and did not die in the wilderness. God promised that this 'restored wife' would soon produce many children.

Discussion Starter 1 reminds us that we should respect God's faithful messengers and the words they bring. We should not surrender to the cynicism that our nation shows towards almost anyone in authority.

'The hand of the enemy' is Christian code. What does it mean to the average non-believer? Use Discussion Starter 2 to make this intelligible. Who is this enemy? How does he hold people prisoner?

Isaiah 54 likens the remnant to an abandoned wife. The Lord will become her husband, restoring her fortunes and comforting her with His love. Discussion Starter 3 invites a pastoral response. How do we avoid using this passage glibly? Stress the need for practical support and fellowship for the bereaved.

Discussion Starter 4 opens up a controversial issue. What is the place of Israel today and what is its relationship to the Church? The next session will shed more light on the matter but this question will reveal where people currently stand on the issue. Don't let the discussion get too heated!

God is always willing to restore the backslidden if they
return with a right heart. Use Discussion Starter 5 to draw
out what this means. Emphasise the need for recognition
of sin, repentance from wrong attitudes and actions,
restitution where appropriate, humility and recommitment.

Humility is not to be equated with weakness. God's people
are to have bite! We are to be confident in God and His
promises. We are on a mission to succeed. Use Discussion
Starter 6 to explore what this means. Be practical.

The worst thing a church can do is to become an inward-
looking cultural enclave. Discussion Starter 7 reminds us
how strongly Jesus feels about us opening our doors to
everyone. This means much more than, 'Well, anyone can
come into our meetings if they want.' If that were true,
then why don't they?

End this session by reading the Personal Application and
the Seeing Jesus sections.

Week 7: The Worldwide Church

Political walls are not first built of bricks and mortar but
of ideas and words. Use this Opening Icebreaker to make
the point. Examples might include eating habits: Jesus
declares all foods clean. Religious rules and regulations:
Jesus fulfilled the Law for us. The chosen and the
rejected: we are all God's elect in Christ.

This session focuses on one of the core truths of
Scripture. Race and grace combined in Abraham but not
in all his descendants. Some of his offspring had faith,
others did not. Some Gentiles had faith. Isaiah foresaw

the day when millions of Gentiles would put their faith in Christ and would become, by grace, sons of Abraham. These 'grafted in ones' (see Rom. 11:17–21) constitute the greater family of the restored desolate woman. Along with believing Jews, they have entered the new covenant and become one glorious holy nation, the Church of Jesus Christ. Salvation has gone global!

To Isaiah this is a great honour for his people and the true point of their servant calling. Salvation is of the Jews and they should rejoice at this transformation of their national status. The merely nationalistic ceases to be the prime concern. Jerusalem is heavenly; the Messiah reigns over all the earth from His place in glory. One day He will return and remake the entire universe. Meanwhile, through the gospel proclamation the holy nation continues to multiply.

Use Discussion Starter 1 to help your people put into their own words the gist of this session so that they could explain it to a Jewish person.

Discussion Starter 2 returns us to the issue of replacement theology versus future restoration theology. Help people understand that the solution lies in the faith continuum between the faithful remnant of Abraham's seed and the Church.

Isaiah foretells the universal proclamation of the gospel, reminding us that we are to reach the whole world. Use Discussion Starter 3 to address what part we can play in ensuring that this happens. Read the Personal Application section at this point.

Temple mentality can grip us all. We erect places of worship, but no house can contain God, and Jesus teaches us that worship will not be confined to dedicated places. Using Discussion Starter 4 ask how this affects our practices and attitudes.

It is easy to use a metaphor like 'light', but what do we mean? Discussion Starter 5 invites us to explain. What kind of enlightenment does Jesus bring? Does it include the abolition of ignorance, for example? Or the removal of spiritual blindness?

The most remarkable gospel fruit in the Early Church was Jews and Gentiles sharing fellowship at a meal table. Cultural and social, religious and racial barriers, were abolished. Explore this and apply it to our own situations using Discussion Starter 6.

Isaiah does not spiritualise earthly Jerusalem and thereby make it less real. Heavenly Jerusalem and the heavenly Temple are the realities upon which the earthly is modelled. That does not make the earthly unimportant or unreal, but it does bring heaven to bear on our earthly existence. We should be people with double vision! Use Discussion Starter 7 to explore how this awareness of the heavenly affects our daily lives.

Hopefully, this study has enlarged the vision of your group and opened their eyes to the greatness of God. Central to Isaiah's message has been God's purpose to bring forth from the faithful remnant His true Servant, the Saviour of the whole world. Finish this session reading the Seeing Jesus section and conclude your studies by focusing on Him in worship and thanksgiving.

National Distributors

UK: (and countries not listed below)
CWR, Waverley Abbey House, Waverley Lane, Farnham, Surrey GU9 8EP.
Tel: (01252) 784700 Outside UK (44) 1252 784700 Email: mail@cwr.org.uk

AUSTRALIA: KI Entertainment, Unit 21 317-321 Woodpark Road, Smithfield, New South Wales 2164.
Tel: 1 800 850 777 Fax: 02 9604 3699 Email: sales@kientertainment.com.au

CANADA: David C Cook Distribution Canada, PO Box 98, 55 Woodslee Avenue, Paris,
Ontario N3L 3E5. Tel: 1800 263 2664 Email: swansons@cook.ca

GHANA: Challenge Enterprises of Ghana, PO Box 5723, Accra. Tel: (021) 222437/223249
Fax: (021) 226227 Email: ceg@africaonline.com.gh

HONG KONG: Cross Communications Ltd, 1/F, 562A Nathan Road, Kowloon.
Tel: 2780 1188 Fax: 2770 6229 Email: cross@crosshk.com

INDIA: Crystal Communications, 10-3-18/4/1, East Marredpalli, Secunderabad – 500026, Andhra
Pradesh. Tel/Fax: (040) 27737145 Email: crystal_edwj@rediffmail.com

KENYA: Keswick Books and Gifts Ltd, PO Box 10242-00400, Nairobi.
Tel: (254) 20 312639/3870125 Email: keswick@swiftkenya.com

MALAYSIA: Salvation Book Centre (M) Sdn Bhd, 23 Jalan SS 2/64, 47300 Petaling Jaya, Selangor.
Tel: (03) 78766411/78766797 Fax: (03) 78757066/78756360 Email: info@salvationbookcentre.com

Canaanland, No. 25 Jalan PJU 1A/41B, NZX Commercial Centre, Ara Jaya, 47301 Petaling Jaya, Selangor.
Tel: (03) 7885 0540/1/2 Fax: (03) 7885 0545 Email: info@canaanland.com.my

NEW ZEALAND: KI Entertainment, Unit 21 317-321 Woodpark Road, Smithfield,
New South Wales 2164, Australia. Tel: 0 800 850 777 Fax: +612 9604 3699
Email: sales@kientertainment.com.au

NIGERIA: FBFM, Helen Baugh House, 96 St Finbarr's College Road, Akoka, Lagos.
Tel: (01) 7747429/4700218/825775/827264 Email: fbfm@hyperia.com

PHILIPPINES: OMF Literature Inc, 776 Boni Avenue, Mandaluyong City.
Tel: (02) 531 2183 Fax: (02) 531 1960 Email: gloadlaon@omflit.com

SINGAPORE: Alby Commercial Enterprises Pte Ltd, 95 Kallang Avenue #04-00, AIS Industrial Building,
339420. Tel: (65) 629 27238 Fax: (65) 629 27235 Email: marketing@alby.com.sg

SOUTH AFRICA: Struik Christian Books, 80 MacKenzie Street, PO Box 1144, Cape Town 8000.
Tel: (021) 462 4360 Fax: (021) 461 3612 Email: info@struikchristianmedia.co.za

SRI LANKA: Christombu Publications (Pvt) Ltd, Bartleet House, 65 Braybrooke Place, Colombo 2.
Tel: (9411) 2421073/2447665 Email: dhanad@bartleet.com

USA: David C Cook Distribution Canada, PO Box 98, 55 Woodslee Avenue, Paris, Ontario N3L 3E5,
Canada. Tel: 1800 263 2664 Email: swansons@cook.ca

CWR is a Registered Charity - Number 294387
CWR is a Limited Company registered in England - Registration Number 1990308

Day and Residential Courses
Counselling Training
Leadership Development
Biblical Study Courses
Regional Seminars
Ministry to Women
Daily Devotionals
Books and DVDs
Conference Centre

Trusted all Over the World

CWR HAS GAINED A WORLDWIDE reputation as a centre of excellence for Bible-based training and resources. From our headquarters at Waverley Abbey House, Farnham, England, we have been serving God's people for over 40 years with a vision to help apply God's Word to everyday life and relationships. The daily devotional *Every Day with Jesus* is read by nearly a million readers an issue in more than 150 countries, and our unique courses in biblical studies and pastoral care are respected all over the world. Waverley Abbey House provides a conference centre in a tranquil setting.

For free brochures on our seminars and courses, conference facilities, or a catalogue of CWR resources, please contact us at the following address:
CWR, Waverley Abbey House, Waverley Lane, Farnham, Surrey GU9 8EP, UK

Telephone: +44 (0)1252 784700
Email: mail@cwr.org.uk
Website: www.cwr.org.uk

CWR Applying God's Word
to everyday life and relationships

Dramatic new resource

2 Corinthians: Restoring harmony
by Christine Platt

Paul's message went against the grain of the culture in Corinth, and even his humility was in stark contrast to Greco–Roman culture. Be challenged and inspired to endure suffering, seek reconciliation, pursue holiness and much more as you look at this moving letter which reveals Paul's heart as much as his doctrine. This thought-provoking, seven-week study guide is great for individual or small-group use.
ISBN: 978-1-85345-551-3

Also available in the bestselling
Cover to Cover Bible Study Series

1 Corinthians
Growing a Spirit-filled church
ISBN: 978-1-85345-374-8

2 Corinthians
Restoring harmony
ISBN: 978-1-85345-551-3

1 Timothy
Healthy churches – effective Christians
ISBN: 978-1-85345-291-8

23rd Psalm
The Lord is my shepherd
ISBN: 978-1-85345-449-3

2 Timothy and Titus
Vital Christianity
ISBN: 978-1-85345-338-0

Ecclesiastes
Hard questions and spiritual answers
ISBN: 978-1-85345-371-7

Ephesians
Claiming your inheritance
ISBN: 978-1-85345-229-1

Esther
For such a time as this
ISBN: 978-1-85345-511-7

Fruit of the Spirit
Growing more like Jesus
ISBN: 978-1-85345-375-5

Genesis 1–11
Foundations of reality
ISBN: 978-1-85345-404-2

God's Rescue Plan
Finding God's fingerprints on human history
ISBN: 978-1-85345-294-9

Great Prayers of the Bible
Applying them to our lives today
ISBN: 978-1-85345-253-6

Hebrews
Jesus – simply the best
ISBN: 978-1-85345-337-3

Hosea
The love that never fails
ISBN: 978-1-85345-290-1

Isaiah 1–39
Prophet to the nations
ISBN: 978-1-85345-510-0

Isaiah 40–66
Prophet of restoration
ISBN: 978-1-85345-550-6

James
Faith in action
ISBN: 978-1-85345-293-2

Jeremiah
The passionate prophet
ISBN: 978-1-85345-372-4

Joseph
The power of forgiveness and reconciliation
ISBN: 978-1-85345-252-9

Mark
Life as it is meant to be lived
ISBN: 978-1-85345-233-8

Moses
Face to face with God
ISBN: 978-1-85345-336-6

Nehemiah
Principles for life
ISBN: 978-1-85345-335-9

Parables
Communicating God on earth
ISBN: 978-1-85345-340-3

Philemon
From slavery to freedom
ISBN: 978-1-85345-453-0

Philippians
Living for the sake of the gospel
ISBN: 978-1-85345-421-9

Proverbs
Living a life of wisdom
ISBN: 978-1-85345-373-1

Revelation 1–3
Christ's call to the Church
ISBN: 978-1-85345-461-5

Revelation 4–22
The Lamb wins! Christ's final victory
ISBN: 978-1-85345-411-0

Rivers of Justice
Responding to God's call to righteousness today
ISBN: 978-1-85345-339-7

Ruth
Loving kindness in action
ISBN: 978-1-85345-231-4

The Covenants
God's promises and their relevance today
ISBN: 978-1-85345-255-0

The Divine Blueprint
God's extraordinary power in ordinary lives
ISBN: 978-1-85345-292-5

The Holy Spirit
Understanding and experiencing Him
ISBN: 978-1-85345-254-3

The Image of God
His attributes and character
ISBN: 978-1-85345-228-4

The Kingdom
Studies from Matthew's Gospel
ISBN: 978-1-85345-251-2

The Letter to the Colossians
In Christ alone
ISBN: 978-1-85345-405-9

The Letter to the Romans
Good news for everyone
ISBN: 978-1-85345-250-5

The Lord's Prayer
Praying Jesus' way
ISBN: 978-1-85345-460-8

The Prodigal Son
Amazing grace
ISBN: 978-1-85345-412-7

The Second Coming
Living in the light of Jesus' return
ISBN: 978-1-85345-422-6

The Sermon on the Mount
Life within the new covenant
ISBN: 978-1-85345-370-0

The Tabernacle
Entering into God's presence
ISBN: 978-1-85345-230-7

The Uniqueness of our Faith
What makes Christianity distinctive?
ISBN: 978-1-85345-232-1

£3.99 each (plus p&p)
Price correct at time of printing

Cover to Cover Every Day
Gain deeper knowledge of the Bible

Each issue of these bimonthly daily Bible-reading notes gives you insightful commentary on a book of the Old and New Testaments with reflections on a Psalm each weekend by Philip Greenslade.

Enjoy contributions from two well-known authors every two months, and over a five-year period you will be taken through the entire Bible.

ISSN: 1744-0114
Only £2.49 each (plus p&p)
£13.80 for annual UK subscription (6 issues)
£13.80 for annual email subscription
(available from www.cwr.org.uk/store)

Cover to Cover Complete
Read through the Bible chronologically

Take an exciting, year-long journey through the Bible, following events as they happened.

- See God's strategic plan of redemption unfold across the centuries
- Increase your confidence in the Bible as God's inspired message
- Come to know your heavenly Father in a deeper way

The full text of the flowing Holman Christian Standard Bible (HCSB) provides an exhilarating reading experience and is augmented by our beautiful:

- Illustrations
- Maps
- Charts
- Diagrams
- Timeline

And key Scripture verses and devotional thoughts make each day's reading more meaningful.

ISBN: 978-1-85345-433-2
Only £19.99 (plus p&p)

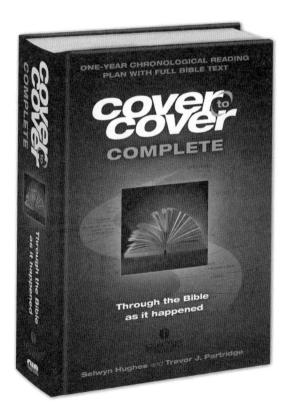